Plants and Flowers

IT'S SCIENCE!

Plants and Flowers

Sally Hewitt

CHILDREN'S PRESS®

A Division of Grolier Publishing

NEW YORK • LONDON • HONG KONG • SYDNEY
DANBURY, CONNECTICUT

Acknowledgments

Bruce Coleman Limited pp. 7tr (Charlie Ott), 7tl, 7c, 12c, 26/27c (Hans Reinhard), 10l (Geoff Dore),
12tl, 14ct (Dr Eckart Pott), 12cl, 20br (Jane Burton), 12cr (Sir Jeremy Grayson), 19bl (John Shaw),
20l, 22bl (Kim Taylor), 21br (Felix Labhardt), 24bl (George McCarthy), 25tr (Robert P. Carr)
NHPA: pp. 7bl (David Woodfall), 14c (GI Bernard), 18tr (EA Janes), 19tr, 19c (Stephen Dalton),
22l (Laurie Campbell), 22tr (GJ Cambridge), 24br (Alan Williams)
OSF: pp. 14l (ER Degginger), 14bc, 22c, 23tr (Bob Gibbons), 18tl (Deni Brown), 18tc (Densey Cline),
18bl, 22br, 25l (Gordon Maclean), 21tr (Rob A. Tyrrel), 25bl (Breck P. Kent)
Holt International Studios: p. 23tl (Nigel Catlin). Thanks to our model, James Moller.

Series editor: Rachel Cooke
Designer: Mo Choy
Picture research: Alex Young
Photography: Ray Moller unless otherwise acknowledged
Series consultant: Sally Nankivell-Aston

Visit Children's Press on the Internet at:
http://publishing.grolier.com

First published in 1998 by Franklin Watts

First American edition 1998 by Children's Press

ISBN 0-516-21176-5 (lib. bdg.)   ISBN 0-516-26341-2 (pbk.)
A CIP catalog record
for this book is available from
the Library of Congress.

Copyright © Franklin Watts 1998

Printed in Malaysia

Contents

Using Plants

Hundreds of the things you use and eat every day come from plants.

The placemat, the loaf of bread, apples, and the table are just some of the things in this picture that come from plants.

Look at the next page to see which plants they come from.

Farmers grow fields of wheat. The **seeds** from the wheat are ground to make flour. We use the flour to make bread.

Wood from tree trunks is used to make furniture.

Apples grow on apple trees.

The placemat is made of cotton. The fluffy cotton bolls that grow on cotton plants are made into cotton thread. The thread is woven together to make cloth.

 THINK ABOUT IT!

Think about the things you use and eat every day. Which of them come from plants?

Growing Plants

Plants need sunlight, air, soil, and water to grow. A gardener makes sure the plants in the garden get these things so they will grow well.

Today Charlie is watering his plants and digging up **weeds**.

 THINK ABOUT IT!

Why do you think Charlie is digging up weeds like this?

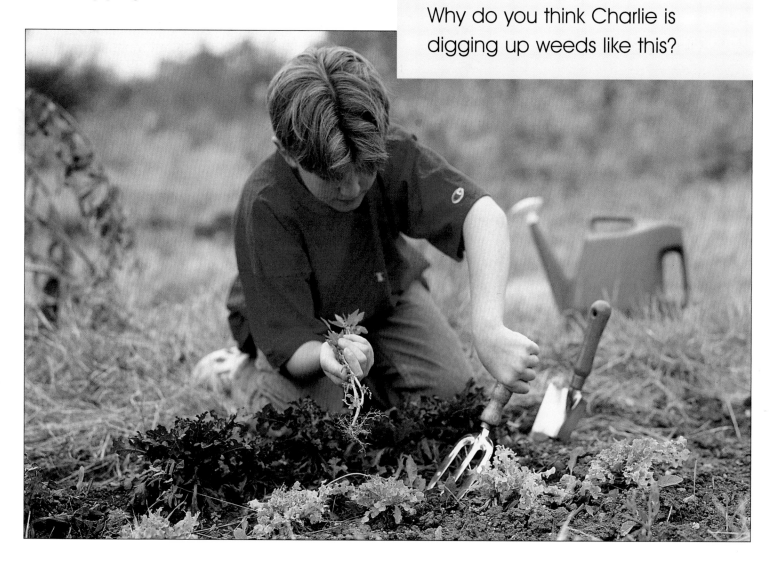

⚕️ TRY IT OUT!

You can grow some plants on cotton wool rather than soil. Try growing mustard in these different ways.

You will need:
- a packet of mustard seeds
- three saucers
- a roll of absorbent cotton
- a cardboard box

Put a layer of cotton in each saucer and sprinkle some mustard seeds on top.

1. With one saucer of seeds, dampen the cotton with water and leave the seeds in the light. Keep the cotton damp over the next six days.

2. With another saucer, leave the seeds in the light, but don't water them.

3. With the last saucer, dampen the cotton and keep it damp but hide the saucer under the box in the dark. Look what happens to the seeds after six days.

💡 THINK ABOUT IT!

Why do you think the seeds in the first saucer grew the best?

Making Food

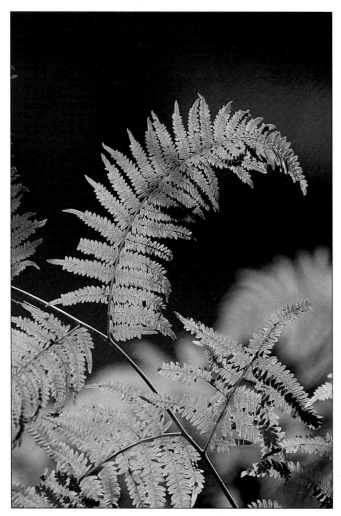

Plants and animals need **energy** from food to live and grow. We eat plants and other animals for food, but plants don't need to eat. They make their own food.

Plants use energy from sunlight, the air all around them, and water from the soil to make food in their green **leaves**.

| seed | root | bulb |

Plants store the food they need to grow in different places, including the **roots** and **stem**.

Seeds and **bulbs** have a store of food so that new plants can grow before they have leaves to make their own food.

 LOOK AGAIN

Look again at page 9. What happens when a plant is kept out of the sunlight?

Water from the soil travels along the roots, up the stem, and into every part of the plant.

TRY IT OUT!
Add some food coloring to a glass of water and put in a white carnation. Watch the **flower** slowly turn blue. Why do you think this happens?

Blood travels through **veins** in your body. Water travels through veins in leaves.

TRY IT OUT!
Collect some leaves. Feel both sides. Lay some white paper over the rough side of a leaf and rub over it with a crayon. Watch the pattern of veins appear.

11

Name the Parts

Not all plants grow flowers, but many of them do.
Some flowers are tiny and difficult to see.
Other flowers are big and brightly colored.

Look at all the different shapes of the
flowers on this page.

TRY IT OUT!

Ask if you can pick some flowers. You will
only need one of each kind. Or, cut out
pictures of flowers from a catalog.
Sort the flowers three different ways—
into colors, then into shapes, and then
into sizes.

Color   Shape

Every part of a plant has a name and a job to do.

We have named the parts of this plant. Every flowering plant, even if it looks very different from the one in the picture, has these parts.

flower

petal

bud

leaf

stem

roots

🖐 TRY IT OUT!

Ask if you can pull up a weed and look at the roots. Name the other parts of the weed as well.

👁 LOOK AGAIN

Look again at page 10 to find a job that a leaf does for a plant.

13

New Plants

Plants start their lives in all kinds of different ways.

A sunflower grows from a seed.

Some new plants grow from tubers under the ground—the potatoes we eat are **tubers**. A new potato plant grows from an old potato.

An onion plant grows from an onion, which is a kind of bulb.

A giant oak tree grows from an acorn. An acorn is a type of seed called a **nut**.

👁 LOOK AGAIN

Look again at page 10. What do seeds, bulbs, and nuts store so that new plants can grow?

TRY IT OUT!

Cut the top off a carrot and put it in a saucer of water.

Fill a glass container with water, and find an onion that fits into the top. Make sure the bottom of the onion is touching the water.

Collect nuts, **fruit** seeds and pits and plant them in some soil.

Leave them in a place with plenty of light, and keep them watered.

Check them every day for signs that they are growing.

Grow a Seed

Beans like these are kinds of seeds. They will grow into a bean plant. New beans that you can pick and eat will grow on the plant.

💡 THINK ABOUT IT!

If you did not eat the new beans, what could you do with them instead? How could you get even more beans?

 TRY IT OUT!

Try growing some beans yourself. You will need:
- a jar
- absorbent cotton
- packet of beans.

16

1. Soak the beans in water over night.

2. Line the jar with cotton. Put a little water in the jar so that the cotton is damp through.

3. Tuck a few of the soaked beans between the cotton and the side of the jar. Keep the cotton damp.

LOOK AGAIN

Look again at page 10. What will the bean plant be able to do once it has grown its green leaves?

4. Watch the root grow downward, searching for water.

5. Watch the shoot grow upward, searching for sunlight.

Pollen

Look inside some flowers and you will see a long thin stalk covered in a yellow powder. The stalk is called a **stamen,** and the yellow powder is called **pollen**.

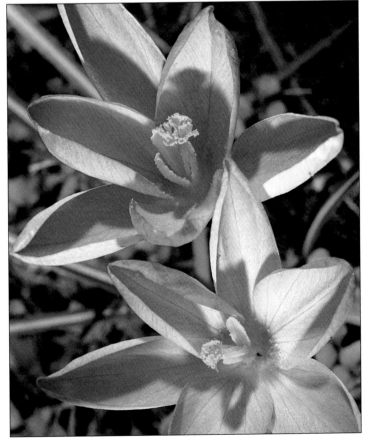

Can you see the long stamens covered in pollen in all these different flowers?

 TRY IT OUT!

Brush your finger on the stamens in a flower and see the pollen on your finger. Be careful—it can stain your fingers and clothes. Pollen also gives some people **hay fever**.

Flowers use pollen to make their seeds. To do this, pollen has to be carried from one flower to another flower. How can this happen when flowers can't move? Something else does the job for them—flying insects, and sometimes even birds and bats.

A bee lands on this dandelion to drink sweet juice called **nectar**. Pollen rubs off onto the bee's back.

The bee flies off carrying the pollen to a new flower. Now this flower will be able to make seeds for a new plant to grow.

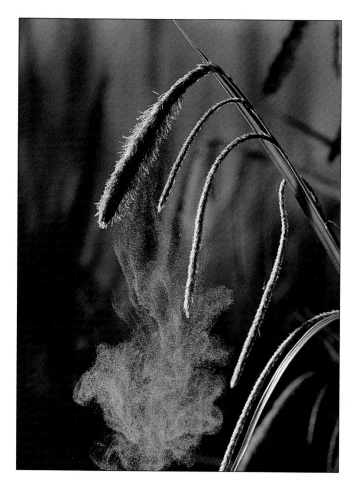

Some plants use the wind to carry pollen. Wind blows sedge pollen from flower to flower.

 THINK ABOUT IT!

Why do you think sedge flowers have to make much more pollen than a dandelion?

19

Come to Dinner

Flowers open out in the warm weather when insects are buzzing around looking for food. The flowers can give them this food.

Most flowers make sugary nectar. Other flowers make extra pollen for the insects to eat. Now they must make sure the insects find them.

Flowers have different ways of inviting insects to come to dinner.

Butterflies visit brightly colored flowers.

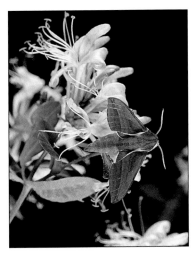

Moths cannot see bright colors because they fly at night. They visit flowers with a sweet smell.

◉ LOOK AGAIN

Look again at page 19 to find out why flowers need insects to visit them.

An iris has guidelines that show insects where to land to find nectar.

Hummingbirds have long beaks to reach for nectar inside brightly colored flowers.

These orchids trick male insects into visiting them by looking just like a female insect!

TRY IT OUT!

Watch flowers on a sunny day and look out for all the different visitors.

21

Fruits and Seeds

When colorful petals have done their job, they die and fall off the flower. Now you can see the fruit forming. The fruit contains the seeds.

Rose petals die, leaving a bright red rose hip. The hip is the fruit. It is full of seeds.

Sunflower heads are packed with striped seeds.

There are thistle seeds inside tiny fruits at the end of each of these fluffy parachutes.

When the orange blossom petals die, tiny oranges start to grow. Pips inside the oranges are seeds.

New chestnut trees grow from shiny nuts.

☀ TRY IT OUT!

Ask an adult to help you cut open fruit from your fruit bowl. Find the seeds and pits inside the fruit.
Can you spot the seeds in all these fruits?

Spreading Seeds

When you buy a packet of seeds, you plant the seeds carefully and make sure they have water and sunlight. Seeds of wild plants have to do this job for themselves.

Fruit and nuts are good to eat, and this can be a good thing for the plant, too.

Birds eat **berries,** and the seeds fall onto the ground in their droppings.

Squirrels bury a store of nuts for the winter and often forget where they are. The birds and squirrels have planted the seeds!

Look at all these other ways
that seeds get spread around.

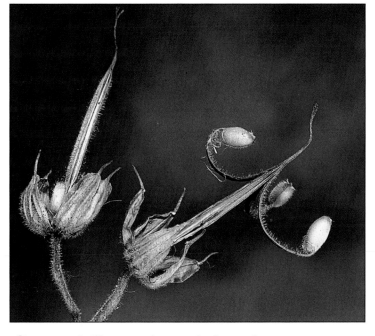

Cranesbill seed pods burst open
when they are touched, and the
seeds shoot out.

Maple seeds
whirl away
from the tree
on wings.

Little hooks on
burrs catch
onto the fur of
a passing
animal and are
carried away.

◉ LOOK AGAIN

Look again at page 22 to find
some seeds that are a good
shape to be blown along by
the wind.

25

Starting Again

Start anywhere on the circle
and follow it around to see
how poppies start
a new life each year.

In the summer, insects visit
the bright red flowers. They
take pollen from one
flower to the next.

In the spring, rainfall and the
warmer weather help the
seed start to grow into a new plant.

The petals drop off, and a head full of seeds is left behind. Wind blows the seed head, and seeds shake onto the ground.

Dirt and leaves cover the seeds in the autumn. The seeds lie under the earth during the cold winter.

 TRY IT OUT!

Plant a bulb (for example, a hyacinth, tulip, or daffodil) in a pot in the autumn. Put the bulb somewhere cool and dark for the winter, and be very patient! In the spring, put the bulb somewhere warm and light, and watch it grow.

Useful Words

Berry Berries, such as strawberries and blueberries, are small juicy fruits with seeds inside them.

Bud New flowers or leaves that are ready to grow are tightly contained inside a bud.

Bulb A bulb is like a bud that grows underground. It is full of food that the new plant needs to grow.

Energy Plants, people, and animals all need energy to grow. They get this energy from food. Plants use energy from the sun to make the food that they need to grow.

Flower Flowers come in all shapes, sizes, and colors. They are the parts of a plant where seeds are formed. New plants will grow from the seeds.

Fruit Fruit contains the seeds of the plant. A cherry is the fruit of a cherry tree; the pit inside is the seed.

Hay fever When some people breathe in pollen, it makes them sneeze and makes their eyes water. If this happens, we say they have an allergy called hay fever.

Leaf A leaf is part of a plant. The green color in a plant's leaves catches the sunlight that the plant needs to make its own food.

Nectar Flowering plants make a sugary liquid food called nectar to attract birds and insects. The animals take pollen from flower to flower as they feed on the nectar.

Nut A nut is a kind of fruit with a seed inside it protected by a hard shell.

Petal Petals are part of a flower. They are a kind of leaf that protects the stamen. They often have bright colors or markings to attract insects.

Pollen Pollen is the yellow dust flowers use to make their seeds. Pollen has to be moved from one flower to another before a seed can form.

Root A root is the part of a plant that reaches down into the soil to collect the water that a plant needs to grow.

Seed A plant grows from a seed. A seed contains a new plant and a store of food for it so that it can begin to grow. The outercase of the seed protects the new plant.

Stamen A stamen is the part of a flower that makes pollen. You often see stamens as long thin stalks covered in pollen in the middle of a flower.

Stem A stem is part of a plant that is usually fairly long and thin. Roots grow from the bottom of the stem into the ground; leaves and flowers grow on the stem above the ground.

Tuber A tuber is a swollen stem that grows underground. It is full of food that the plant needs to grow.

Vein You can see the veins in leaves. Veins are thin tubes that carry water and food through a plant.

Weed Weeds are what gardeners and farmers call plants that grow where they don't want them to.

Index

About This Book

Children are natural scientists. They learn by touching and feeling, noticing, asking questions, and trying things out for themselves. The books in the *It's Science!* series are designed for the way children learn. Familiar objects are used as starting points for further learning. *Plants and Flowers* starts with food on a table and explores plants and how they grow.

Each double-page spread introduces a new topic, such as insects and pollen. Information is given, questions asked, and activities suggested that encourage children to make discoveries and develop new ideas for themselves.
Look for these panels throughout the book:

TRY IT OUT! indicates a simple activity, using safe materials, that proves or explores a point.
THINK ABOUT IT! indicates a question inspired by the information on the page but that points the reader to areas not covered by the book.
LOOK AGAIN introduces a cross-referencing activity that links themes and facts through the book.

Encourage children not to take the familiar world for granted. Point things out, ask questions, and enjoy making scientific discoveries together.